## REPTILES

# IGUANAS

BY SHANNON JADE

# WWW.APEXEDITIONS.COM

Copyright © 2024 by Apex Editions, Mendota Heights, MN 55120. All rights reserved. No part of this book may be reproduced or utilized in any form or by any means without written permission from the publisher.

Apex is distributed by North Star Editions:
sales@northstareditions.com | 888-417-0195

Produced for Apex by Red Line Editorial.

Photographs ©: Shutterstock Images, cover, 1, 4–5, 7, 10–11, 12, 14–15, 16–17, 20–21, 22–23, 24, 26–27, 29; iStockphoto, 6, 8–9, 13, 18, 19

Library of Congress Control Number: 2022920184

**ISBN**
978-1-63738-546-3 (hardcover)
978-1-63738-600-2 (paperback)
978-1-63738-705-4 (ebook pdf)
978-1-63738-654-5 (hosted ebook)

Printed in the United States of America
Mankato, MN
082023

## NOTE TO PARENTS AND EDUCATORS

Apex books are designed to build literacy skills in striving readers. Exciting, high-interest content attracts and holds readers' attention. The text is carefully leveled to allow students to achieve success quickly. Additional features, such as bolded glossary words for difficult terms, help build comprehension.

### CHAPTER 1
### AN ESCAPE 4

### CHAPTER 2
### TYPES OF IGUANAS 10

### CHAPTER 3
### IGUANA DIETS 16

### CHAPTER 4
### LIFE CYCLE 22

**COMPREHENSION QUESTIONS • 28**
**GLOSSARY • 30**
**TO LEARN MORE • 31**
**ABOUT THE AUTHOR • 31**
**INDEX • 32**

# CHAPTER 1

# AN ESCAPE

An iguana rests high up in a tree. The iguana is hungry. So, it looks for food. It spots some tasty leaves nearby.

Many iguanas have long toes and sharp claws. They are good at climbing trees.

**Hawks use their strong eyesight to hunt small animals.**

The iguana takes a big bite. Its sharp teeth shred the leaves. Suddenly, a hawk swoops down toward the tree. It tries to eat the iguana.

FAST FACT
Iguanas have strong jaws and sharp teeth. This helps them chew tough food.

Different types of iguanas eat different types of leaves.

The hawk grabs the iguana's tail. But the tail falls off! The iguana scurries away to safety. It won't be eaten today.

# TERRIFIC TAILS

When iguanas are in danger, they can detach their tails. Losing their tails can help iguanas escape **predators**. The tails can grow back later.

It can take two to twelve months for an iguana's tail to grow back.

**CHAPTER 2**

# Types of Iguanas

Iguanas are **reptiles**. There are many different iguana **species**. The most common is the green iguana. Green iguanas live in rain forests.

Green iguanas have a line of spikes down their backs.

Some iguanas live in deserts. They are found in Mexico and the United States. These iguanas have **adapted** to hot temperatures. Their bodies are good at saving water.

Many desert iguanas are tan and brown. These colors help them blend in with rocks and sand.

Creosote bushes can grow in dry, sandy areas.

## CREOSOTE BUSHES

Desert iguanas mostly live in areas where creosote bushes grow. Iguanas eat this bush's flowers. They hide in its leaves and branches. They even sleep underneath it.

**Marine** iguanas live on beaches in the Galápagos Islands. They can dive more than 65 feet (20 m) underwater. They also spend time resting in the sun on rocks.

## FAST FACT

Marine iguanas can spend up to 30 minutes underwater.

A marine iguana's dark-colored scales help it warm up after swimming.

CHAPTER 3

# IGUANA DIETS

Most iguanas are **herbivores**. They eat fruit, leaves, and flowers. Some iguanas have **bacteria** inside their bodies that help break down their food.

Iguanas often eat hibiscus flowers.

**Even iguanas that eat insects mainly eat plants.**

However, iguanas sometimes eat other food. They might eat insects or snails. Some types of iguanas eat bird eggs, too.

FAST FACT

Marine iguanas eat **algae** that grows on ocean rocks.

Marine iguanas may dive deep to find algae and seaweed.

Animals such as snakes and owls hunt iguanas. But iguanas move quickly. Their teeth, claws, and tails are sharp. They can often fight back or escape.

Iguanas sometimes hold still to avoid being seen by predators.

## JUMP TO SAFETY

Iguanas are good at jumping and swimming. They can use these skills to escape predators. An iguana in a tree may leap into the water to get away.

CHAPTER 4

# LIFE CYCLE

Some types of iguanas live in groups. Others live alone. But all come together to **mate**. Male iguanas try to attract females by flicking their tongues and bobbing their heads.

Male iguanas may fight one another during mating season.

After mating, female iguanas lay eggs. They dig to bury the eggs in dirt or sand. These spots are usually warm. Then female iguanas leave the eggs alone.

## TROUBLE FOR IGUANAS

Iguanas are becoming less common in the wild. Humans build on the land where iguanas live. Some people also hunt iguanas or capture them as pets.

◀ **Iguanas dig nests to keep their eggs warm.**

The eggs hatch a few months later. Baby iguanas dig their way out. They can live on their own right away.

All the eggs in a nest usually hatch around the same time.

**FAST FACT**
Some species of iguana can live for up to 60 years.

# COMPREHENSION QUESTIONS

Write your answers on a separate piece of paper.

1. Write a sentence describing the food iguanas usually eat.

2. Iguanas can live in rain forests, in deserts, or on islands. Which place would you prefer to live? Why?

3. What type of iguana lives in the rain forest?
    A. green iguana
    B. desert iguana
    C. marine iguana

4. How might jumping into water help iguanas escape predators?
    A. Iguanas can't move quickly on land.
    B. The predators might move faster in water.
    C. The predators might not be able to swim.

**5.** What does **detach** mean in this book?

*When iguanas are in danger, they can **detach** their tails. Losing their tails can help iguanas escape predators.*

    **A.** shake something back and forth
    **B.** make something grow bigger
    **C.** make something fall off

**6.** What does **bury** mean in this book?

*They dig to **bury** the eggs in dirt or sand.*

    **A.** cover up
    **B.** throw away
    **C.** turn off

*Answer key on page 32.*

# GLOSSARY

**adapted**
Changed to fit a new situation.

**algae**
Tiny plant-like living things that are found in the water.

**bacteria**
Tiny living things that can help break down food.

**herbivores**
Animals that eat mostly plants.

**marine**
Related to the sea.

**mate**
To form a pair and come together to have babies.

**predators**
Animals that hunt and eat other animals.

**reptiles**
Cold-blooded animals that have scales.

**species**
Groups of animals or plants that are similar and can breed with one another.

## BOOKS

Murray, Julie. *Iguanas*. Minneapolis: Abdo Publishing, 2020.

Perish, Patrick. *Collared Lizards*. Minneapolis: Bellwether Media, 2019.

Ringstad, Arnold. *Totally Amazing Facts about Reptiles*. North Mankato, MN: Capstone Press, 2018.

## ONLINE RESOURCES

Visit **www.apexeditions.com** to find links and resources related to this title.

## ABOUT THE AUTHOR

Shannon Jade writes both fiction and nonfiction books. She lives in Australia alongside some of the world's greatest landscapes and most amazing animals.

# INDEX

**A**
algae, 19

**B**
bacteria, 16
bite, 6–7

**C**
creosote bushes, 13

**D**
deserts, 12–13

**E**
eggs, 25–26

**G**
Galápagos Islands, 14
green iguana, 10

**H**
habitats, 12–14
herbivores, 16

**M**
marine iguana, 14–15, 19
mating, 22, 25

**P**
predators, 8–9, 20–21

**R**
rain forests, 10
reptiles, 10

**T**
tails, 8–9, 20
teeth, 6–7, 20

**ANSWER KEY:**
1. Answers will vary; 2. Answers will vary; 3. A; 4. C; 5. C; 6. A